MW00988695

Georgia Courthouse Disasters

Paul K. Graham

The Genealogy Company
Decatur, Georgia

Georgia Courthouse Disasters

© 2013, Paul K. Graham

The Genealogy Company
P.O. Box 1091
Decatur, Ga. 30031-1091

ISBN-13: 978-0-9755312-9-7
ISBN-10: 0-9755312-9-8

LCCN: 2013931714

More information:
www.pkgraham.com/courthouse

From the Author

Courthouse fires never mean all is lost. Records always survive. Fire-proof vaults saved many records from destruction. Some fires burned slow and material was saved. Clerks took books home to work at night. Court offices were in a separate building. Copies of records were sent to the state or federal government for various purposes. Even when courthouse records were almost completely consumed, records created by families, organizations, corporations, and other governmental jurisdictions can fill gaps. Working around record destruction can be challenging, but all is not lost.

About the Author

Paul K. Graham, CG, AG, is a professional genealogist whose expertise lies in documenting families of the U.S. South. His books and articles about Georgia records and families have been recognized with awards from the Georgia Genealogical Society, American Society of Genealogists, and National Genealogical Society. He holds a master's degree in Heritage Preservation from Georgia State University and resides in Salt Lake City, Utah.

Introduction

Genealogists and historians regularly face the problem of record destruction. Few places in the United States feel this type of loss like the state of Georgia. Over its history, 75 of the state's counties have suffered 109 events resulting in the loss or severe damage of their courthouse or court offices. Many endured significant record loss and its aftereffects. This is problematic because counties maintain three of the most important records for documenting the lives of Georgia's citizenry: deeds, estates, and marriages.

The purpose of this book is to document the destruction of Georgia county courthouses from 1777 to today, including the date, time, circumstance, and impact on records. Not all of those details could be proved for every courthouse disaster. Because county boundaries change over time, maps are included showing the areas impacted by each fire that destroyed records.

Previously, cursory lists only gave a hint of destructive events and potential loss of records. None were complete, and many included dates of planned demolitions or "fires" that never happened. Through careful research, each event has now been documented using contemporary evidence. If a courthouse disaster does not appear in this book, no evidence was found during the research process.

Like all efforts of this kind, the book does have limitations. It does not address destruction of colonial records during the Revolutionary War, nor does it speak to losses of state records. It does not reflect fires in city halls. Although considered, a full accounting of all surviving county records was not made. That worthy effort will be extraordinarily time consuming. All of these items fall outside the scope of this work. Even the included vignettes are purposely limited and could be expanded with further research. Corrections and additions for the author are welcome, as long as they are submitted with conclusive evidence from contemporaneous source documents.

Undocumented Record Loss

Some record loss events remain unexplained. Two counties with the most undocumented record loss are Bryan and Union. Bryan County probate records were destroyed in 1866. According to a short county history written by Joseph L. Buhler, Sr., the ordinary moved his records to his private residence, which then burned shortly after. No known records mention the event.

Union County is missing numerous pre-Civil War records, including deeds to 1860, court minutes to 1855, and probate minutes to 1851. No mention of these losses has been found in contemporary records. In fact, the county grand jury repeatedly noted the good condition of the records from 1857 to 1865. In October 1865, they reported: "We are happy to say our books are in as good [a] condition as could be reasonabl[y] expected in the present and former distracted condition of the county."

Maps

For counties where record losses affect an area beyond the current boundaries, maps are included to show the extent of the impact on records. Each map shows modern county boundaries along with areas of maximum impact (boundaries at the time of the fire) and limited impact (areas previously part of the county). This is important for researchers because many fires affect places outside the current county boundaries. The underlying data used to create the boundary maps comes from the Atlas of Historical County Boundaries, published by the Newberry Library. All impact maps are presented at 1:2,000,000 scale, or approximately 30 miles per inch.

Genealogical Research Strategies

Despite record losses in many courthouses across the country, it is possible to overcome the gaps using fundamental research strategies. While many of the events of people's lives can never be fully reconstructed, details can be gleaned from other records to piece together families and the arcs of individual lives. Records created after the courthouse loss, or by other government jurisdictions, or by private organizations, all reveal important details about people. For researchers, a courthouse disaster does not necessarily mean a dead end. It means broadening the field of research.

Broaden the search to other jurisdictions. Land, military, and tax records created or copied by the state and federal governments are the most common sources used to fill in gaps created by courthouse disasters, but many other types of records exist. For urban dwellers, seek out city records.

Broaden the search to private entities. Newspapers hold vast amounts of historical information. Church records may provide evidence of residence and vital dates. Business records, such as a store ledger, could lead to clues.

Broaden the search to other repositories, like libraries, historical societies, and archives. Identify those that collect records relevant to whatever county is involved. Remember that collections may be limited by subject rather than geography, such as the archives of a religious sect. A comprehensive research guide—such as the revised edition of *Georgia Research: A Handbook for Genealogists, Historians, Archivists, Lawyers, Librarians, and Other Researchers*— will provide details about records, jurisdictions, and repositories beyond the county courthouse.

Broaden the search by expanding the research techniques. Look to friends, neighbors, and extended family. Study migration patterns to learn about the family before and after they lived in the burned county. Methodically disprove possible relationships to narrow the list of probable relationships.

Alphabetical List of Georgia Courthouse Disasters

Appling	1876
Baker	1873, 1925, 1994
Baldwin	1861
Bartow (Cass)	1864
Bulloch	1864
Burke	1856
Butts	1828, 1864
Calhoun	1891, 1920
Carroll	1928
Charlton	1878, 1928
Cherokee	1864, 1927
Clayton	1864
Clinch	1856, 1867
Cobb	1864
Coffee	1898, 1938
Colquitt	1881
Crawford	1830
Dade	1853, 1863
Decatur	1878
DeKalb	1842, 1916
Dooly	1847
Dougherty	1940, 1966
Douglas	1956
Echols	1897
Emanuel	1841, 1919, 1938
Fannin	1936
Fayette	1982
Forsyth	1973
Glynn	1896
Gordon	1888, 1888
Grady	1980
Greene	1787

Gwinnett	1871
Habersham	1923
Hall	1851, 1882, 1936
Hart	1900, 1967
Heard	1839, 1894
Jefferson	1864
Jenkins	1910
Lee	1858
Lowndes	1858, 1870
Macon	1857
Marion	1845
McIntosh	1863, 1873, 1931
Meriwether	1893, 1976
Miller	1873, 1873, 1904, 1974
Mitchell	1867
Morgan	1844
Muscogee	1838
Newton	1883
Oconee	1887
Paulding	1864
Pickens	1947
Pierce	1875
Polk	1864
Quitman	1921
Screven	1864, 1897
Seminole	1922
Spalding	1981
Stewart	1922
Talbot	1892
Telfair	1934
Toombs	1917
Troup	1936
Twiggs	1901

Walker	1883
Ware	1874
Warren	1854, 1909
Washington	1855, 1864
Webster	1914
Wheeler	1916
Wilcox	1878
Wilkes	1958
Wilkinson	1828, 1854, 1864, 1924
Worth	1879, 1880, 1893, 1982

Chronological List of Georgia Courthouse Disasters

Greene	1787	September
Butts	1828	February 1
Wilkinson	1828	March 16
Crawford	1830	February 18
Muscogee	1838	October 8
Heard	1839	April 14
Emanuel	1841	May 10
DeKalb	1842	January 19
Morgan	1844	September 1
Marion	1845	November 4
Dooly	1847	May 7
Hall	1851	December 20
Dade	1853	April 15
Wilkinson	1854	February 7
Warren	1854	April 23
Washington	1855	March 24
Burke	1856	January 24
Clinch	1856	June
Macon	1857	February 25

Lee	1858	March 19
Lowndes	1858	June 23
Baldwin	1861	February 24
McIntosh	1863	June 11
Dade	1863	November
Clayton	1864	August 19
Bartow	1864	October
Cherokee	1864	October
Jefferson	1864	November
Polk	1864	November 1 or 2
Paulding	1864	November 2 or 3
Cobb	1864	November 13
Butts	1864	November 17
Wilkinson	1864	November 23–26
Washington	1864	November 27
Screven	1864	December 2–3
Bulloch	1864	December 5
Mitchell	1867	January 7
Clinch	1867	September
Lowndes	1870	November
Gwinnett	1871	September 12
Miller	1873	January 6
McIntosh	1873	January 25–26
Baker	1873	December 17–18
Miller	1873	December 23
Ware	1874	October 12–13
Pierce	1875	March 11
Appling	1876	September 7
Wilcox	1878	March 30–31
Charlton	1878	May
Decatur	1878	May 6
Worth	1879	January 26–27
Worth	1880	October 24

Colquitt	1881	February 25
Hall	1882	January 2–3
Walker	1883	February 2
Newton	1883	December 31
Oconee	1887	January 7
Gordon	1888	March 20
Gordon	1888	October 23
Calhoun	1891	December 11
Talbot	1892	February 12
Meriwether	1893	March 3
Worth	1893	August 9
Heard	1894	March 10
Glynn	1896	September 29
Screven	1897	January 8
Echols	1897	December 31
Coffee	1898	October 13
Hart	1900	December 25
Twiggs	1901	February 7
Miller	1904	October 9
Warren	1909	April 6
Jenkins	1910	January 16
Webster	1914	September 27
Wheeler	1916	March 9
DeKalb	1916	September 13
Toombs	1917	November 21
Emanuel	1919	May 22
Calhoun	1920	August 2
Quitman	1921	February 1
Seminole	1922	March
Stewart	1922	April 21
Habersham	1923	December 1
Wilkinson	1924	February 15
Baker	1925	January

Cherokee	1927	March 10
Carroll	1928	February 4
Charlton	1928	February 19
McIntosh	1931	March 23
Telfair	1934	February 10
Hall	1936	April 6
Fannin	1936	July 2
Troup	1936	November 5
Emanuel	1938	November 10
Coffee	1938	November 25
Dougherty	1940	February 10
Pickens	1947	February 4
Douglas	1956	January 11
Wilkes	1958	December 24
Dougherty	1966	May 2
Hart	1967	January 6
Forsyth	1973	November 5
Miller	1974	December 2
Meriwether	1976	January 27
Grady	1980	February 18
Spalding	1981	January 2
Worth	1982	January 27
Fayette	1982	April 11
Baker	1994	July

The Appling County courthouse at Baxley burned in the early morning of September 7, 1876. By the time flames were discovered about 1 a.m., nothing could be done to extinguish the fire. Most county records were lost, but the deed books survived.

The county seat had been moved from Holmesville four years earlier, and the Baxley courthouse was about three years old. A replacement courthouse—this time brick instead of wood—was not finished until the fall of 1885. Although mentioned in multiple twentieth-century sources, no evidence points to a courthouse fire in the 1850s.

"Courthouse Burned," Macon *Telegraph and Messenger*, September 9, 1876, p. 4.
Georgia Laws, January Session 1873, 216.
Georgia Laws, January Session 1874, 378–379.
"The News in Georgia," Macon *Weekly Telegraph*, October 13, 1885, p. 11.

Baker County's courthouses at Newton have suffered fire and floods. The most disastrous event came during the night of December 17 and 18, 1873. The ordinary had left from work without putting out the fire in his office. By the time his error was discovered fifteen minutes before 1 a.m., the fire consumed the interior of the courthouse.

Ordinary court records and most of the superior court records were destroyed in the blaze. Among the surviving books were Deed Book 20 and mortgage books B and C. An 1845 county tax digest not stored in the courthouse also survived.

The courthouse constructed after the 1873 fire was replaced in 1900. The new building would see the Flint River flood Newton multiple times over the course of the twentieth century, including 1925, 1929, 1944, 1966, 1994, and 1998. Of those, the threat to

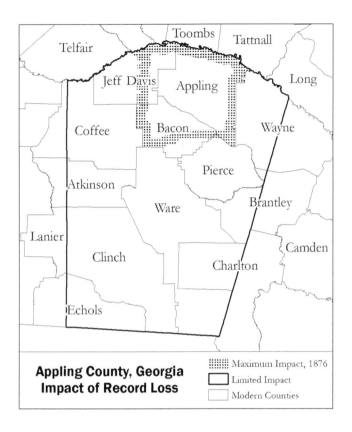

Appling County, Georgia
Impact of Record Loss

▦ Maximum Impact, 1876
☐ Limited Impact
☐ Modern Counties

the courthouse was most dire in 1925 and 1994. Although no longer used as the courthouse, the building still stands.

The 1925 flood began on Monday, January 19 when the Flint River overran its banks and water rushed through Newton. The river rose quickly, reaching thirty-six feet by the next day. The flood's crest moved through the town on Thursday night, January 22, at more than forty-one feet. Water stood eight feet deep on the town square, flooding the first floor of the courthouse. All of Newton's residents had been evacuated during the previous week. Initially, Sheriff R. L. Griffin and Mrs. Ida May Cox, the postmistress, remained, occupying the second story of the courthouse, but they were evacuated as the water rose.

In 1994, tropical storm Alberto passed over western Georgia, creating the worst flooding in the region in recorded history. Flood waters crested in Baker County on Thursday, July 12, at just over forty-five feet. Downtown Newton was covered in more than sixteen feet of water.

"A Court-House Burned," Macon *Georgia Weekly Telegraph and Journal and Messenger*, December 23, 1873, p. 3.

"Flood-Tracking Chart for the Flint River Basin, Georgia," U.S. Department of the Interior, U.S. Geological Survey, Open-File Report 01-325.

"Flint at Standstill at Albany," Atlanta *Constitution*, January 21, 1925, p. 5.

"Heavy Losses in Water's Wake," Atlanta *Constitution*, January 26, 1925, p. 2.

" Newton Has Food but No Beds for Evacuees," Marietta *Daily Journal*, July 11 1994, p. 5.

"Newton," Marietta *Daily Journal*, July 12, 1994, p. 8.

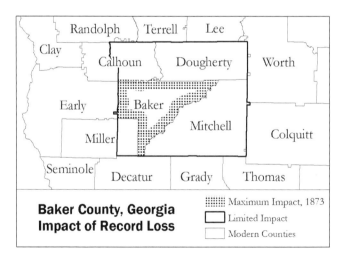

Baldwin

The Baldwin County courthouse in Milledgeville was set on fire by an unknown person early in the morning on Sunday, February 24, 1861. Flames were discovered between 4 and 5 a.m. and the building was entirely consumed by 7 a.m. The arsonist started the fire in the superior court office, and all records of that court were destroyed. Records of the ordinary court and sheriff's office were saved.

"Court House Burnt," Milledgeville *Southern Recorder*, February 26, 1861, p. 3.

**Baldwin County, Georgia
Impact of Record Loss**

Maximum Impact, 1861
Limited Impact
Modern Counties

The Cass County (now Bartow County) courthouse was destroyed by federal forces during the Civil War. On October 30, 1864, a detail of 250 men from the Fifth Ohio Volunteer Cavalry was ordered to burn Cassville, after allowing the citizens to remove their effects.

The exact circumstances are not known, but many records were saved from destruction. Some marriages, deeds, and estates preceding the Civil War were preserved. Unfortunately, a significant amount of county records did not survive.

Official Records, Armies, Ser. I, Vol. XXXIX, Pt. III, 513.

Federal troops making their way through Statesboro during the March to the Sea destroyed the Bulloch County courthouse on December 5, 1864. The march across Georgia took thirty-five days, from November 15, 1864, in Atlanta to December 20 in Savannah. By the time federal troops reached Bulloch County, the greater part of the Army of the Tennessee was moving as one body toward the coast.

On December 4, elements of the Second and Third divisions of the Fifteenth Army Corps met with resistance from Confederate troops on the outskirts of Statesboro, the county seat. Two engagements reported at the time resulted in quick losses and retreat by the defenders. By the evening of the December 4, the Second and Third divisions were camped in the town.

The two divisions left Statesboro at dawn on December 5. They were likely in the town for less than sixteen hours. In addition to the loss of numerous Confederate soldiers in the previous day's skirmishes, the Bulloch County courthouse was also destroyed. David Beasley, the county ordinary, made a notation in his minute book on December 5. "This being the day appointed by law for holding the court of ordinary of said county, but the Yankees was here and at States Borough and burned the court house on that day. As such there was no court held." Although some records were affected, the vast majority of the county's books survived the war.

Official Records, Armies, Ser. I, Vol. XLIV, 118–120, 620–621, 630.
Bulloch Co., Ordinary Court, Minutes, 1858–1867: 142.

Some time around midnight on Thursday, January 24, 1856, a fire broke out in the Burke County courthouse in Waynesboro. The building burned to the ground, taking with it the vast majority of county  records. Some dwellings, stores, and offices in the immediate proximity of the courthouse were also destroyed, but the fire was stopped before it could spread across the whole town. Although some books dating to the 1830s were saved, Burke County's record losses are considered among the worst in Georgia.

Numerous twentieth-century sources point to a courthouse disaster in 1825, but the event is not corroborated in contemporary records. In fact, what documents do speak about the courthouse strongly suggest that a new building was planned and constructed about that time. On December 8, 1818, the Georgia legislature authorized Burke County to collect an extra tax for the purpose of building a courthouse. The tax would continue until the cost of construction was collected. Then on May 16, 1821, the legislature authorized the sale "of a certain lot of land belonging to said county, in the town of Waynesborough, on which the old Court-house is situated." Unfortunately, the

1856 fire eliminated the crucial court records that could tell about events in the 1820s.

"Fire in Waynesboro," Macon *Georgia Telegraph*, February 5, 1856, p. 2.

Lucius Q. C. Lamar, Esq., *Compilation of the Laws of the State of Georgia...1810 to the year 1819...* (Augusta: T. S. Hannon, 1821), 916.

Georgia Laws, April and May Session 1821, 28–29.

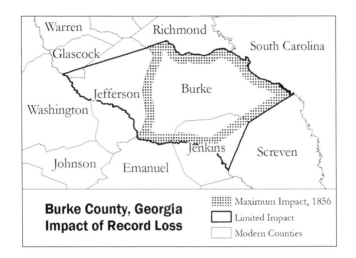

Burke County, Georgia
Impact of Record Loss

Maximum Impact, 1856
Limited Impact
Modern Counties

The unfinished Butts County courthouse at Jackson burned during the night of February 1, 1828. The county had been organized two years before, on December 24, 1825. Foul play was not involved; a newspaper reported that the flames "were communicated by accident." Because the building was not yet occupied, county records were not affected.

On November 17, 1864, divisions of the Fifteenth and Seventeenth corps passed through Jackson on Sherman's March to the Sea. They left the courthouse and jail in ruins. The records were

17

saved from destruction, and the first grand jury after the war commended county officers on the books' condition.

"Fire," Macon *Telegraph*, February 11, 1828, p. 3.
Official Records, Armies, Ser. I, Vol. XLIV, 478–480.
Butts Co., Superior Court, Minutes, 1865-1873: 17–18.

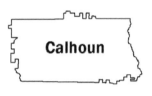

The Calhoun County courthouse at Morgan was destroyed by fire on the night of Friday, December 11, 1891. The vast majority of county records survived due to the use of a modern fire-proof vault. The fire spurred an effort by the town of Arlington to have the new courthouse built there, but the county seat would remain in Morgan.

In the wake of the 1891 fire, a new wooden courthouse was constructed at a cost of $6,000. Around 1:30 a.m. on the morning of Monday, August 2, 1920, a fire was discovered in the sheriff's office at the courthouse by a woman who was awake taking care of one of her children. She woke her husband and he roused the town, but nothing could be done. It only took an hour for flames to bring down the structure. Except for documents in the sheriff's office, the county records remained safe in the fire-proof vault.

"Calhoun County News," Macon *Telegraph*, December 17, 1891, p. 7.
"Calhoun Court House Burned," Macon *Daily Telegraph*, August 3, 1920, p. 14.
"Court House Destroyed," Macon *Daily Telegraph*, August 4, 1920, p. 4.

Flames were discovered in the Carroll County courthouse at 1 a.m. on Saturday, February 4, 1928. Over the next four hours, the Carrollton fire department battled the blaze, but it had progressed too far by the time firemen arrived. By 5 a.m. the courthouse had been destroyed. Fire-proof vaults minimized record loss.

"Flames Destroy Carroll County Courthouse," Atlanta *Constitution*, February 4, 1928, p. 10.

The Charlton County courthouse burned not long before May 16, 1878. Surviving county records do not specify the exact date. The first deed recorded after the fire was entered in the record book on July 2, 1878.

Charlton

Three months from the fiftieth anniversary of the 1878 fire, the next courthouse was destroyed by fire. On the afternoon of February 19, 1928, a fire started between the courthouse roof and the ceiling. By the time it was discovered, it had advanced too far to be extinguished. However, the blaze moved slow, allowing time to remove county records and courthouse furniture.

"The Georgia Press," Macon *Telegraph and Messenger*, May 16, 1878, p. 2.
Charlton Co., Deed Book A: 7-8.
"Charlton County Court House Razed with $20,000 Loss," Atlanta *Constitution*, February 20, 1928, p. 14.

Cherokee

The Cherokee County courthouse at Canton was destroyed by federal forces during the same operation that led to the destruction of the Bartow County courthouse on or about October 30, 1864. Unlike in Bartow, a significant amount of the county's records were saved from the fire. Losses of the earliest marriage and probate records likely occurred during this event. The county deed books survived intact.

A new courthouse was completed in 1874 and was used for almost fifty-three years before it too burned down. On the evening of March 10, 1927, a fire was discovered in the upper story of the courthouse. By the time the alarm went out, the blaze could not be brought under control. A newspaper account placed the time of destruction at 10 p.m., although it did not clarify whether that was when the fire was discovered or when firefighters gave up the fight. The county's books were not protected by a fire-proof vault, but there was enough time for people to carry them to safety.

Official Records, Armies, Ser. 1, Vol. XXXIX, Pt. III, 513.
"Cherokee County Courthouse Destroyed by Fire," Canton *Cherokee Advance*,
   March 11, 1927, p. 1.

Federal troops under the command of General Armstrong and General Kilpatrick destroyed the Clayton County courthouse at Jonesboro during their occupation of the town on August 19, 1864. In a report of items burned there, a provost marshal reported the following statistics: bales cotton (96), depot (1), courthouse (1). The county's records were removed in advance of the military assault.

Official Records, Armies, Ser. I, Vol. XXXVIII, Pt. II, 858, 862.
"Clayton's Court House," Atlanta *Constitution*, March 5, 1886, p. 7.

Clinch County lost two courthouses to fire. Existing documents only provide limited accounts, and no evidence to clarify the dates has been located.

An arsonist destroyed the county courthouse in 1856, likely in June. Bids for construction of a new building were advertised beginning on July 8. In December, with the new courthouse finished, the Clinch County grand jury noted that six months had passed since the fire.

In the late summer of 1867—likely in September—the next courthouse burned. The grand jury called for the September term of Superior Court lamented that losing the courthouse came at a particularly difficult time, only two years after the end of the Civil War. None of the county's records survived.

"Clinch Superior Court—December Term, 1856," Milledgeville *Southern Recorder*, March 3, 1857, p. 3.
"Notice," Milledgeville *Federal Union*, July 8, 1856, p. 3.
Clinch Co., Superior Court, Minute Book A: 2, 14.

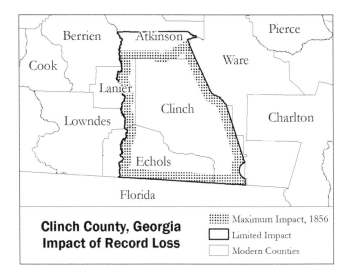

Clinch County, Georgia
Impact of Record Loss

▦ Maximum Impact, 1856
☐ Limited Impact
☐ Modern Counties

In advance of the arrival of federal troops in Marietta during the summer of 1864, Cobb County's records were moved out of the county for safe keeping. They ended up in Social Circle, sixty miles southeast. There they were destroyed, likely a few days prior to July 25, 1864, by Union cavalry under the command of General Garrard. The

courthouse burned on November 13, 1864, starting about noon. Attempts to save the structure failed.

Official Records, Armies, Ser. I, Vol. XXXVIII, Pt. V, 248, 250.

Cobb Co., Superior Court, Minute Book A: 34.

Marching with Sherman: Passages from the Letters and Campaign Diaries of Henry Hitchcock, ed. M. A. DeWolfe Howe (1927, reprint, Lincoln: University of Nebraska Press, 1995), 52.

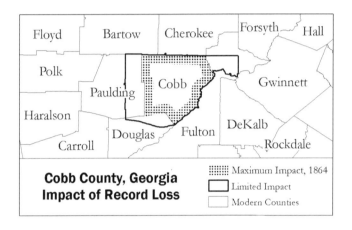

Cobb County, Georgia
Impact of Record Loss

Two Coffee County courthouses at Douglas have burned. The first fire occurred on Friday night, October 13, 1898, destroying the building and many of the county's earliest records. The Democrats blamed the Populists for setting the fire in order to destroy votes from the October 5th election for governor, thus forcing a new election. Allen D. Candler, the Democrat, would win the election over Populist J. R. Hogan by a margin of forty percent. The county's deed records survive, while most probate records survive only from the 1870s.

The replacement courthouse survived thirty-eight years before its destruction in the early morning hours of November 25, 1938. According to the sheriff, who discovered the fire, the blaze started under the roof in the rear of the building. The exact cause was not determined, although there was no indication of arson. The county's records were protected by a fire-proof vault.

"Votes Were Burned," Savannah *Tribune*, October 15, 1898, p. 4.

"Courthouse Burns in Coffee County," Atlanta *Constitution*, November 26, 1938, p. 10.

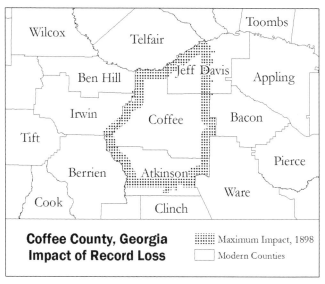

Coffee County, Georgia
Impact of Record Loss

▓▓ Maximum Impact, 1898
☐ Modern Counties

Colquitt

On Friday night, February 25, 1881, Colquitt County's courthouse at Moultrie burned to the ground. With few exceptions, the county's records were destroyed. The fire was blamed on arson, because the fireplaces and stoves had not been used for a month. The Colquitt fire was not an isolated event, and the Albany *News and Advertiser* worried that the Irwin County courthouse would be next—but no fire was set there.

"The Georgia Press," Macon *Georgia Weekly Telegraph and Journal and Messenger*, March 4, 1881, p. 2.

The Crawford County courthouse at Knoxville was destroyed by an arsonist on Thursday night, February 18, 1830. The former superior court judge was initially suspected, but not enough evidence could be found to charge him. Probate and land records were destroyed, but the marriage book survived. A law passed in December 1832 incorrectly states that the fire occurred in 1829.

"Fire," Macon *Georgia Messenger*, February 20, 1830, p. 3.
Georgia Laws, November and December Session 1832, 109–110.

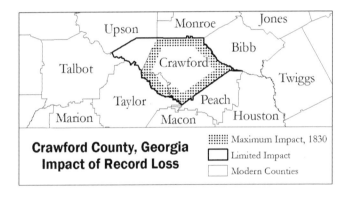

Crawford County, Georgia
Impact of Record Loss

Maximum Impact, 1830
Limited Impact
Modern Counties

The Dade County courthouse at Trenton was destroyed twice in ten years. On April 15, 1853, the courthouse and all of its contents were destroyed by fire. Brief newspaper mentions do not explain how the fire started.

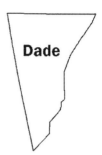

Ten years later, federal infantry moved through Dade County in the days leading up to the Battle of Missionary Ridge. The Third Division, Fifteenth Corps, commanded by General Hugh Ewing, occupied Trenton from November 19 to November 21, 1863, destroying numerous iron works in the area. By the time they left, the entire town of Trenton lay in ruins. When the county's grand jury convened a year later, they found "our public buildings destroyed and most of our county records gone."

The two fires wreaked havoc on the records. Almost nothing survived the 1853 fire. The 1863 fire destroyed all probate records, including marriages. Superior court records fared only slightly better, with two deed books and the court minutes saved.

Milledgeville *Federal Union*, April 26, 1853, p. 3.

"Destruction of a Court-House in Georgia by Fire," New York *Times*, April 19, 1853, p. 1.

Official Records, Armies, Ser. I, Vol. XXXI, Pt. III, 185–186.

Official Records, Armies, Ser. I, Vol. XXXI, Pt. II, 584–589.

"From Upper East Tennessee," Augusta *Daily Chronicle and Sentinel*, November 26, 1863, p. 2.

"Doings of the Yankees in Dade Co.," Athens *Southern Banner*, February 24, 1864, p. 3.

Dade Co., Superior Court, Minute Book B: 5–7.

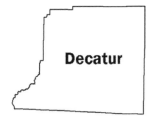

Decatur

The Decatur County courthouse at Bainbridge was burned by arsonists on May 6, 1878. A $100 reward was offered for the arrest and conviction of the parties. Many records survived, including deeds, but the probate court suffered heavy losses.

"Georgia News," Columbus *Daily Enquirer-Sun*, May 14, 1878, p. 3.

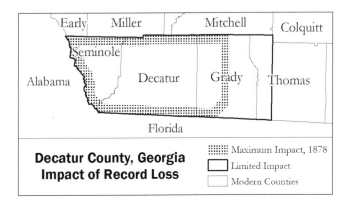

Decatur County, Georgia Impact of Record Loss

Maximum Impact, 1878
Limited Impact
Modern Counties

Two DeKalb County courthouses have been destroyed by fire. The first destructive event occurred on the night of January 19, 1842. All records excepting two minute books—one each from the superior court and inferior court—were lost in the blaze.

DeKalb

A later courthouse suffered a fire in the early morning hours of September 13, 1916. Flames were discovered about 5 a.m. and could not be stopped. The interior was gutted. Multiple theories were expressed concerning the cause of the fire, but none were substantiated.

School records and the papers of the summer court sessions were destroyed, but the county records stored in a fire-proof vault survived. The exterior of the building survived and the interior was rebuilt with a new roof. Although not used for court purposes, the courthouse still stands in Decatur.

"Fire!," Milledgeville *Federal Union*, February 1, 1842, p. 2.
"DeKalb Courthouse Destroyed by Blaze," Atlanta *Constitution*, September 14, 1916, p. 9.

DeKalb County, Georgia
Impact of Record Loss

On the night of Friday, May 7, 1847, the Dooly County courthouse at Vienna was set on fire, destroying the building and its contents. In addition to public records, the county

sheriff had placed as much as $12,000 in the courthouse for safe-keeping. Newspaper accounts alluded to the fact that the fire may have been set in order to destroy evidence that the money was stolen. It was a huge sum in that day. A one-thousand-dollar reward was offered for the conviction of the arsonists, but no one was ever charged.

"Court House Burnt," Macon *Georgia Telegraph*, May 18, 1847, p. 2.

"Dooly Court Hourt [*sic*] Burnt," Milledgeville *Southern Recorder*, May 18, 1847, p. 3.

"$1000 Reward!," Milledgeville *Federal Union*, July 27, 1847, p. 4.

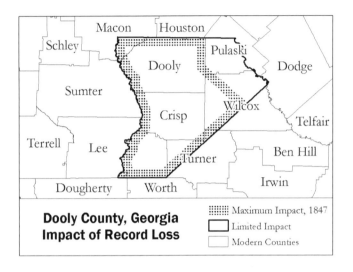

Dooly County, Georgia
Impact of Record Loss

▒▒▒▒ Maximum Impact, 1847
☐ Limited Impact
☐ Modern Counties

The Dougherty County courthouse narrowly escaped destruction by a powerful tornado that killed more than twenty people in downtown

Dougherty

Albany early in the morning of 10 February 1940. The force of the twister caused considerable interior damage, and the county's set of law books had to be replaced. In 1966, the county offices were being moved out of the courthouse in preparation for the structure's demolition. In the evening of Monday, May 2, 1966, a fire started on the upper floor of the courthouse, but was brought under control by firefighters. Some documents were damaged, but the most important county records were not affected.

"Albany Tornado Kills Score, Hurts 300; Damage $5,000,000," Augusta *Chronicle*, February 11, 1940, p. 1.

Georgia Laws, 1943, 1708–1709.

"Dougherty Courthouse Burns," Marietta *Daily Journal*, May 3, 1966, p. 3.

The Douglas County courthouse burned in the early morning of January 11, 1956. The fire was discovered about 5 a.m. By the time volunteer firefighters got the call, the building could not be saved. Fire-fighting efforts concentrated on surrounding buildings, including the city hall and a church. Firemen from Marietta, Atlanta, Austell, and Villa Rica eventually joined the fight. The cause of the fire was believed to be a basement furnace that exploded. The building was entirely gutted, and only the outer walls remained standing. Most county records were protected in fire-proof vaults and safes.

"Flames Gut Douglasville Courthouse," Marietta *Daily Journal*, January 11, 1956, p. 1.

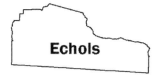

Arsonists destroyed the original Echols County courthouse in Statenville around midnight, Friday, December 31, 1897. It was a wood structure constructed in 1859, the year after the county was formed. The safe in the clerk of court's office was open, leading to suspicion that the perpetrators had meant to rob the court. However, no money was in the safe, and other reports suggested that the intent was to destroy county records.

A buggy was seen leaving the scene prior to the flames being discovered. It was tracked through the woods, showing that the driver had taken a wild course in order to avoid being followed. At least two people were suspected, but there was not enough evidence to bring charges. The fire did its work, destroying almost all of the county's records. Deed books B and E survived along with some wills dating from 1875.

"Court House Consumed," Macon *Telegraph*, January 5, 1898, p. 3.
"Echols' Courthouse Burned," Atlanta *Constitution*, January 5, 1898, p. 3.

Emanuel County courthouses at Swainsboro have been destroyed by fire three times in the county's history. The first fire, on May 10, 1841, destroyed the courthouse. Most of the county's records were lost, but a significant amount still survive.

Another courthouse burned in the early morning hours of May 22, 1919. The cause was not determined. All of the superior court and ordinary court records were kept in an annex building and were not affected by the fire. Records of the county commission kept in a vault were not seriously damaged.

The third courthouse fire in Emanuel County occurred during the first hours of November 10, 1938. It was discovered about midnight, and it took fire crews until 3 a.m. to gain control. Fire crews from Laurens and Bulloch counties were called in to assist with the fight. The county's records were stored in a vault.

Although claimed in some modern accounts, no courthouse disasters occurred in 1855 and 1857. A new courthouse was authorized in January 1853 and completed by John A. Stevenson by October 1855. The supposed fires were not mentioned in newspapers during that period. The superior, inferior, and ordinary courts continued their business uninterrupted, and their minutes make no mention of a disaster or new construction.

"Fire at Swainsborough," Milledgeville *Federal Union*, May 11, 1841, p. 2.

Emanuel Co., Superior Court, Minutes 1851–1859.

Emanuel Co., Inferior Court, Minutes 1841–1859: 17, 111, 114.

Emanuel Co., Ordinary Court, Minutes 1841–1857.

"Court House Burns," Macon *Daily Telegraph*, May 23, 1919, sec. 2, p. 10.

"Courthouse Swept by Fire in Emanuel," Atlanta *Constitution*, November 11, 1938, p. 5.

![Emanuel County, Georgia map showing Impact of Record Loss]

Emanuel County, Georgia
Impact of Record Loss

::::: Maximum Impact, 1841
▢ Modern Counties

The Fannin County courthouse in Blue Ridge was destroyed by fire early in the morning of July 2, 1936. A collection of Georgia law books burned, but the county's records were protected by a fire-proof vault.

"Fannin Court House Destroyed By Fire," Marietta *Journal*, July 2, 1936, p. 7. Georgia Laws, 1937, 1403–1404.

The third floor of the Fayette County courthouse in Fayetteville was gutted when arsonists firebombed the building on Sunday, April 11, 1982. The blaze caused the bell tower to collapse into the third floor, but the first two floors suffered little damage. County records stored in basement vaults were unharmed.

"Fire Enemy of Old Courthouses," Atlanta *Constitution*, April 13, 1982, p. 1C. New York *Times*, April 14, 1982, p. A18.

Just after 10 p.m. on November 5, 1973, flames erupted in the Forsyth County courthouse at Cumming. By the time the fire was brought under control about 2:30 a.m. the next day, the 71-year-old building was completely destroyed. The blaze quickly

engulfed the building, and witnesses reported smelling gasoline. Many loose records were destroyed, including those in the offices of the superior court clerk, ordinary (probate court), tax commissioner, and justice of the peace. However, most of the county's books were stored in fire-proof vaults and survived.

"Fire Levels Courthouse," Marietta *Daily Journal*, November 6, 1973, p. 2.

In the early morning hours of September 29, 1896, a hurricane made landfall at Cedar Key, Florida, on the gulf coast. Tracking northeast, the center of the storm passed over the western edge of Glynn County, producing strong 100-mile-per-hour sustained winds across the county. Damage was severe, and newspapers reported $500,000 of losses in Brunswick alone.

The Glynn County courthouse, an already-dilapidated wooden structure, suffered significant damage but did not collapse like witnesses expected. The courthouse was called a source of mortification, and calls for a new building began immediately after the storm. Except for limited water damage, county records were not affected by the storm.

"Disaster in Brunswick," Atlanta *Constitution*, September 30, 1896, p. 1.
"Brunswick is Building Up," Atlanta *Constitution*, October 2, 1896, p. 1.
"Brunswick is Short on Tin," Atlanta *Constitution*, October 3, 1896, p. 2.
Al Sandrick, "The September 29th, 1896 North Florida Hurricane," in Florida
   Governor's Hurricane Conference (National Weather Service, 2012).

The Gordon County courthouse suffered two disasters in 1888. At about 11 p.m. on the night of March 20, a tornado tore through the busi-  ness section of Calhoun, completely wrecking the center of town. The courthouse, a brick structure, was damaged beyond repair. Its east end was blown out and part of the roof was ripped off.

While the county began the process of building a new court-house, an existing building was converted for use by the superior court, sheriff, and county commissioners. That building was con-sumed by flames in the early morning hours of October 23, only seven months after the tornado. The fire originated in the *Calhoun Times* newspaper office as a result of a defective flue. The newspaper building was consumed and the fire spread to other businesses. As a heavy rain poured down and the fire threatened the temporary courthouse, citizens carried the county records to safety.

"The Cyclone in Calhoun," Macon *Weekly Telegraph*, March 27, 1888, p. 3.
"The Calhoun Fire," Macon *Telegraph*, October 25, 1888, p. 3.
"By Cyclone and Fire," Atlanta *Constitution*, October 24, 1888, p. 2.

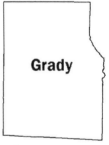

Grady County's courthouse at Cairo, built in 1907, was destroyed by an early-morning blaze on Monday, February 18, 1980. The fire started on the third floor and took almost seven hours to extinguish. As interior supports weakened, the roof collapsed, bringing the heavy dome crash-ing down to the ground floor. Firefighters and citizens removed many county records, and most historical documents were protected in vaults.

"Grady Courthouse Burns," Augusta *Chronicle*, February 19, 1980, sec. B, p. 5.
"Landmark Destroyed," Marietta *Daily Journal*, February 19, 1980, p. 9.

The town of Greensboro, county seat of Greene County, was completely destroyed by a Creek raiding party in September 1787. Attacks on multiple forts were reportedly precipitated by the killing of Indians by whites in the preceding

months. The raids had been anticipated and residents evacuated to Wilkes County carrying the small amount of official county records with them. Greene County had been created on 3 February 1786, but courts were not organized for another year. The Georgia legislature authorized the construction of a county courthouse and jail on 10 February 1787. Although not described in contemporary records, it was almost certainly a small wood structure built in the spring or summer that year.

Robert Watkins and George Watkins, *Digest of the Laws of the State of Georgia...* (Philadelphia: R. Aitken, printer, 1800), 359–361.

Letter of Timothy Barnard, August 18, 1787, Box 1, Folder 11, Document 8, Telamon Cuyler Collection, Hargrett Rare Book and Manuscript Library, University of Georgia Libraries, presented in the Digital Library of Georgia.

Charleston (S.C.) *Columbian Herald*, November 2, 1787, p. 1.

"New York," Maryland *Journal and Baltimore Advertiser*, December 18, 1787, p. 2.

A purported gang of men set fire to the Gwinnett County courthouse at Lawrenceville shortly after midnight the morning of September 12, 1871. As flames consumed the building, men on horseback headed away from the town shouting and shooting pistols. A

man previously charged with a criminal offense was arrested nearby with a revolver and a box of matches. The fire moved too quickly to allow anything to be saved, and almost all of the county's records were destroyed.

"Destructive Conflagration," Atlanta *Constitution*, September 12, 1871, p. 1.
"The Georgia Press," Macon *Georgia Weekly Telegraph and Journal and Messenger*, September 19, 1871, p. 4.

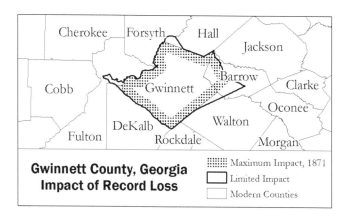

Gwinnett County, Georgia
Impact of Record Loss

Maximum Impact, 1871
Limited Impact
Modern Counties

Just before midnight on December 1, 1923, a fire started in the Habersham County courthouse at Clarkesville. It spread quickly through the second-floor courtroom. The fire department fought the blaze into the early hours of December 2, keeping it from spreading to nearby buildings. A constant stream  of water on the record vault helped save the county's records.

The county is missing numerous early probate records. The first will book was destroyed in the 1923 fire. The cause of other missing books is unclear. Estate inventories date from 1863. Probate bonds survive from 1881.

"$50,000 Is Loss As Courthouse Is Razed by Fire," Atlanta *Constitution*, December 3, 1923, p. 2.

Hall

Hall County courthouses have been destroyed three times in the county's history. An alarm was sounded at 2 a.m. on Friday, December 20, 1851, when fire was discovered at Lemuel McAfee's smoke house in Gainesville. A strong wind that night added fuel and the blaze quickly spread, first catching Mitchell's hotel. From there, the fire spread in multiple directions, destroying the entire downtown section, including the courthouse. Only the walls remained standing. Enough time lapsed between the alarm and the fire reaching the courthouse that the county records could be removed.

Another courthouse burned following New Year's celebrations in 1882. The fire started some time during the night of January 2 to 3. Blame was placed on embers from roman candles that had been launched the previous night. The county records were saved.

The third courthouse disaster in Hall County came with two cataclysmic tornados that ripped through the business section of Gainesville at 7:30 p.m. on April 6, 1936. More than 200 people were killed, another 1,000 injured, and property losses were estimated to exceed $5 million. As one newspaper account stated, "the courthouse was blown wide open." Photographs show the roof and second floor of the building completely missing. For the third time, the county's records survived a potential disaster.

"The Fire in Gainesville," Savannah *Daily Republican*, December 27, 1851, p. 2.
"Georgia News," Columbus *Daily Enquirer-Sun*, January 5, 1883, p. 3.
"150 Are Known Dead at Gainesville," Atlanta *Constitution*, April 7, 1936, p. 1.

On the afternoon of December 25, 1900, the Hart County courthouse at Hartwell burned to the ground. The county's records survived. Seven years earlier, on June 25, 1893, the same building had been damaged when the roof was ripped off by a tornado.

After 1900, the county built a new yellow-brick courthouse. It survived until the night of January 6, 1967, when it too was destroyed by fire. The blaze started about 10:30 p.m. on the upper floor. Fire departments from Hartwell and eight other towns battled through the night to control the fire and save nearby structures. More than 1,000 spectators gathered to watch.

"Hartwell, 1893," HRT-056, Vanishing Georgia, Georgia Archives.
"Hart Courthouse Burned," Atlanta *Constitution*, December 26, 1900, p. 10.
"The Big Hart Fire," Athens *Daily News*, January 8, 1967, p. 1.
"Hart County Courthouse Burns," Augusta *Chronicle-Herald*, January 8, 1967, sec. A, p. 6.

Heard County courthouses at Franklin have been burned to the ground twice in the county's history. The first occurred on the night of April 14, 1839 and the second on the morning of March 10, 1894. Both were set by arsonists. Between them, the fires consumed almost seventy years of county records.

Milledgeville *Federal Union*, April 30, 1839, p. 3.
Georgia Laws, 1839, 194.
Heard Co., Ordinary Court, Minutes Book 1: 3.
Georgia Laws, 1894, 277.
Marietta *Journal*, March 22, 1894, p. 8.

During the Civil War, the Fourteenth Corps passed through Louisville, the county seat of Jefferson County, from November 29 to December 1, 1864, on its way to Savannah. The courthouse was "defaced by the Enemy," but it was not burned. In May 1865, the county grand jury reported that the courthouse had bad locks, and repairs should be made immediately. Although probate and tax records survive, all of the county's deed books were lost during the war. The earliest surviving deed was recording on February 20, 1865.

Official Records, Armies, Ser. I, Vol. XLIV, 56–57.
Jefferson Co., Deed Book A: 41–42.
Jefferson Co., Superior Court, Minutes 1864-1872: 38–40.

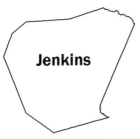

The Jenkins County courthouse at Millen was completely destroyed by fire at 8 p.m. on January 16, 1910. The fire originated in the city court office, where live coals fell from a grate. The county's records, stored in fire-proof vaults, survived.

"Court House at Millen Was Burned," Macon *Daily Telegraph*, January 16, 1910, p. 2.

The Lee County courthouse at Leesburg was destroyed by fire on March 19, 1858. Almost all of the county's records burned.

"Court House Burnt," Columbus *Enquirer*, March 23, 1858, p. 2.

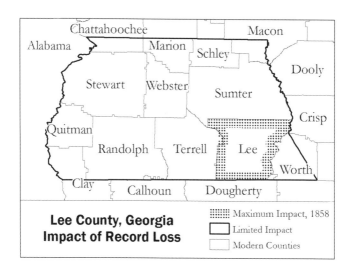

Lee County, Georgia
Impact of Record Loss

▦ Maximum Impact, 1858
☐ Limited Impact
☐ Modern Counties

Lowndes

The Lowndes County courthouse at Troupville burned early in the morning of June 23, 1858. Fire was discovered between 2:30 and 3 a.m. By then flames had engulfed the upper story and nothing could be done to save the structure. Within an hour, the building was completely consumed. Captain James M. Folsom, a lawyer visiting from Magnolia, personally saved many probate records. Because the fire started near the clerk's office, deeds and other superior court records were destroyed.

The county ordinary's office (now probate court) at Valdosta was destroyed by fire in the fall of 1870 following a scandal over contracting for a new courthouse. The details of events—full of intrigue and too involved to fully recount here—are told in grand jury presentments. The grand jury recommended a new court-house be built as early as May 1868. During 1869, the ordinary W. G. Smith fraudulently mismanaged the contractor bidding process, leading to a year-long confrontation with other county

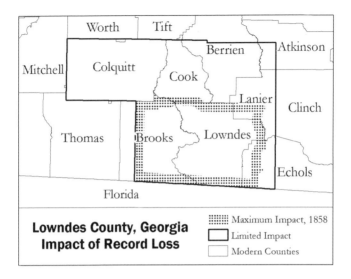

**Lowndes County, Georgia
Impact of Record Loss**

▦ Maximum Impact, 1858
☐ Limited Impact
☐ Modern Counties

leaders. By May 1870, the grand jury was repeatedly stressing the need for a new courthouse, and they noted the urgency of selling the old courthouse, which was quickly deteriorating.

During this period, county officers maintained offices in other buildings in Valdosta. Sometime in November 1870, the ordinary's records were completely destroyed by fire, a fact mentioned in court minutes in December. By then, W. H. Dasher had replaced Smith in the position. The destruction may have come as part of a large fire that swept downtown Valdosta on November 8, taking ten buildings and numerous offices. However, no newspaper accounts mention losses by the ordinary on that night.

Construction on the courthouse finally began in 1871. Work progressed slowly due to a general lack of funds during the decade following the Civil War. The building was complete by spring 1874, and finishing touches were put in place by the fall. Completion of the new courthouse was made official by the grand jury in November 1874.

"Lowndes Court House Burnt," Macon *Georgia Telegraph*, June 29, 1858, p. 3.

"Correspondence of the Savannah Republican," Macon *Georgia Telegraph*, June 29, 1858, p. 3.

"Disastrous Fire at Valdosta," Macon *Georgia Weekly Telegraph and Journal and Messenger*, November 15, 1870, p 2.

Lowndes Co., Superior Court, Minute Book A: 512, 583, 600, 621.

Lowndes Co., Superior Court, Minute Book B: 17, 41, 114, 366, 406.

At about midnight on the night of February 25, 1857, fire destroyed the Macon County courthouse at Oglethorpe. Arson was suspected because no fire had been lit in the building during the preceding week. The entire upper portion of the building was engulfed before being discovered. Except for a small number of probate records, the county's records burned.

"Fire in Oglethorpe," Milledgeville *Southern Recorder*, March 3, 1857, p. 3.

Fire was discovered at the Marion County courthouse at Tazewell about 1:30 a.m. on the morning of November 4, 1845. The blaze was blamed on arson, since the courthouse stove had not been lit since the previous winter. The building and almost all of the county's records were destroyed.

"Another," Augusta *Daily Chronicle and Sentinel*, November 13, 1845, p. 2.

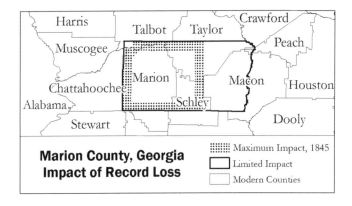

Marion County, Georgia
Impact of Record Loss

▦ Maximum Impact, 1845
☐ Limited Impact
☐ Modern Counties

Federal troops looted and destroyed Darien, county seat of McIntosh County, during the day on June 11, 1863. Soldiers approached the town by boat just before noon, shelling it briefly before landing. Citizens had already evacuated the town, removing many of their belongings. Most of what remained was taken by the raiding party, and the town was set on fire. The courthouse, with almost every other structure in the town, was destroyed.

Whether county records were evacuated or destroyed in 1863 is not clear from available accounts. However, a fire on the night of January 25 and 26, 1873, destroyed almost all that may have remained. The courthouse and its contents were lost.

The courthouse built to replace the one burned in 1873 has suffered two fires. A blaze on the night of March 23, 1931, severely damaged the building and required major renovations. In the morning of December 7, 1981, someone firebombed the courthouse causing smoke damage. County records were not affected in either incident.

Official Records, Armies, Ser. I, Vol. XXVIII, Pt. II, 11–13.

"The Burning of Darien," Augusta *Daily Chronicle and Sentinel*, June 20, 1863, p. 2.

"The Destruction of Darien," Macon *Daily Telegraph*, June 20, 1863, p. 2.

"The Destruction of Durien [*sic*]," Savannah *Daily Morning News*, June 26, 1863, p. 2.

Russell Duncan, *Blue-Eyed Child of Fortune: The Civil War Letters of Colonel Robert Gould Shaw* (Georgia: University of Georgia Press, 1992), 341–345.

"Fire at Darien," Macon *Georgia Weekly Telegraph and Journal and Messenger*, February 4, 1873, p. 8.

Georgia Laws, January to March 1931, 131.

"Bomb Damages Boise School," Kennewick (Wash.) *Tri-City Herald*, December 8, 1981, Valley Section.

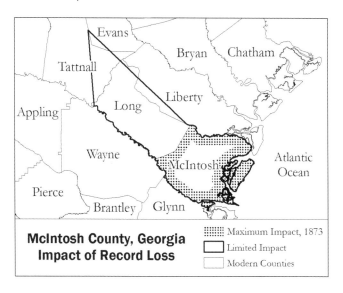

McIntosh County, Georgia
Impact of Record Loss

Meriwether

The town of Greenville, county seat of Meriwether County, was severely damaged by a tornado that touched down about 8:30 p.m. on March 3, 1893. Many houses were demolished, trapping their occupants in the rubble. Despite the potential for high loss of life, only one person was reported dead. The storm severely damaged the courthouse, rendering it unsafe for use, but no records were significantly affected.

Meriwether County's next courthouse served until 1976, when, on the afternoon of January 27, 1976, it was gutted by fire. A crew of local inmates were stripping paint during a renovation, and one of them accidentally dropped a cigarette into a flammable liquid. The county's records were protected in vaults.

"The Cyclone," Columbus *Enquirer-Sun*, March 5, 1893, p. 7.
"Fire Guts Courthouse," Marietta *Daily Journal*, January 28, 1976, p. 3.

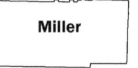

Miller County has suffered four courthouse fires, leaving no official records pre-dating 1870 and significant gaps through 1904. The first fire occurred on the night of January 6, 1873. It destroyed the courthouse at Colquitt with all its contents, including county records. Less than a year later, on Tuesday night, December 23, 1873, the replacement courthouse was set on fire, again destroying the contents.

An arsonist destroyed the next courthouse about 3 a.m. the morning of October 9, 1904. The Colquitt town marshal discovered and extinguished a fire in the building at 1 a.m., then returned home. Within two hours, the arsonist returned. By the time the second blaze was discovered, the courthouse could not be saved. Many of the county's records were destroyed, leaving gaps from 1874 to 1904.

A fourth fire occurred in 1974. Flames were discovered near the courthouse roof at about 10:30 p.m. on December 2. The building could not be saved.

"The Georgia Press," Macon *Telegraph and Messenger*, January 14, 1873, p. 2.
Macon *Telegraph and Messenger*, December 27, 1873, p. 2.
"Fire Destroys Legal Temple," Atlanta *Constitution*, November 10, 1904, p. 5.
"Courthouse Destroyed," Waycross *Journal-Herald*, December 3, 1974, p. 1.

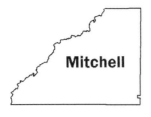

The Mitchell County courthouse at Camilla burned on January 7, 1867. Probate records were destroyed. The superior court clerk saved the books of his office, including all the deeds.

"News and Other Items," Milledgeville *Federal Union*, January 22, 1867, p. 2.
"History of Thomas County," Thomasville *Daily Times Enterprise*, December 20, 1920, p. 3.

On September 1, 1844, the Morgan County courthouse at Madison was destroyed by fire. No cause was reported in newspapers. All of the county's records were saved.

Milledgeville *Georgia Journal*, September 10, 1844, p. 2.

In 1838, Muscogee County was in the process of building a new courthouse in Columbus. The old building was located in the middle of Courthouse Square, and offices of the superior and inferior courts were in ante-buildings on the same block. At around 3 a.m. on October 8, 1838, an arsonist set fire to the courthouse, and within an hour the building was consumed. The fire jumped to the court offices, destroying those buildings as well. With a few exceptions, the county's records burned.

"Eventful Morning," Milledgeville *Federal Union*, October 30, 1838, p. 1.

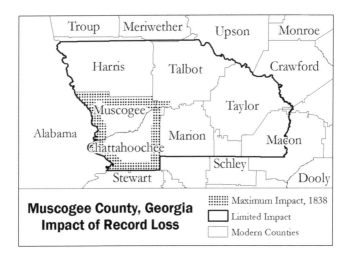

**Muscogee County, Georgia
Impact of Record Loss**

▦ Maximum Impact, 1838
☐ Limited Impact
☐ Modern Counties

At about 8:20 p.m. on December 31, 1883, a fire started in the storeroom at Bagby's barroom in Covington, county seat of Newton County. It was caused by a defective stove flue. The fire spread quickly, jumping to other buildings, lighting the courthouse and consuming six other businesses. Fire

Newton

crews took two hours to bring the blaze under control. When it became clear that the courthouse was going to burn, citizens carried the county's records to safety. "A few old tax books and old files of court records" burned.

"Covington, Georgia," Atlanta *Constitution*, January 1, 1884, p. 2.
Atlanta *Constitution*, January 2, 1884, p. 2.
"Covington, Georgia," Atlanta *Constitution*, January 2, 1884, p. 2.

Oconee

At about midnight on January 7, 1887, a fire was lit in the stairwell of the building occupied by Arnold's drug store and Shackleford's printing office in Watkinsville, seat of Oconee County. Press reports suggested that two or three people were involved in the arson, and their tracks were found in the snow. Fueled by drugs and printing equipment, the blaze quickly consumed the building.

As the fire began spreading through the business district, judge R. M. Jackson and a local minister began carrying the county court's books from the courthouse. Other people asked why they were going to all this trouble—the courthouse would not burn. In the end, the judge made the right decision, because the little blue building suffered the same fate as most of Watkinsville.

Records of the other courts were kept in separate buildings near the courthouse. Citizens covered the small structures with blankets, soaking them with snow and water. The only office to lose all its record was the county commission. Watkinsville was almost completely destroyed in one of the most destructive fires in Georgia history. In an ironic twist, the town had voted to build a waterworks only a week before the fire.

"Destroyed by Fire," Atlanta *Constitution*, January 9, 1887, p. 6.
"Fire," Athens *Weekly Banner-Watchman*, January 11, 1887, p. 3.
"Oconee Court House Destroyed By Fire," Atlanta *Constitution*, May 7, 1938, p. 17.

Paulding County's courthouse at Van Wert was destroyed during the Civil War on November 2 or 3, 1864. After destroying Cedartown in Polk County, the Seventeenth Army Corps moved to Van Wert during the morning of November 2. The

Paulding

47

courthouse and some buildings were burned. The county's records were destroyed, with the exception of a small number of important books. Deeds remain from 1851, superior court minutes survive from 1859, and the ordinary was able to save one will book and a book of letters of administration.

Official Records, Armies, Ser. I, Vol. XXXIX, Pt. III, 579, 597–599.

Tom Hightower to his Wife, November 28, 1864, New Market, Va., in Mills Lane (ed.), *"Dear Mother: Don't Grieve About Me. If I Get Killed, I'll Only be Dead.": Letters from Georgia Soldiers in the Civil War* (Savannah: Beehive Press, 1977), 337–338.

"From Rome," Macon *Daily Telegraph and Confederate*, December 7, 1864, p. 1.

Paulding Co., Superior Court, Minute Book A: 276–277.

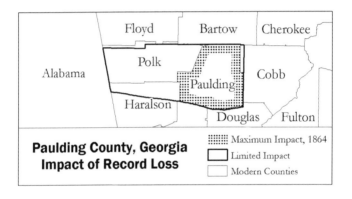

Paulding County, Georgia Impact of Record Loss

▦ Maximum Impact, 1864
▢ Limited Impact
▢ Modern Counties

Fire destroyed the Pickens County courthouse at Jasper early in the morning of February 4, 1947. Under a cold, steady rain, a traveler in town discovered the blaze around 4 a.m. The cause was attributed to defective wiring in the 60-year-old building. The vast majority of the county's records survived the fire.

"Pickens County Courthouse Burns," Marietta *Daily Journal*, February 4, 1947, p. 1.

An arsonist destroyed the Pierce County courthouse at Blackshear about 2 a.m. on March 11, 1875. The fire started under the courthouse, and reports suggested that kerosene or turpentine were used as an accelerant.  The blaze spread across the entire city block, destroying seven businesses and several residences. Almost all of the county's records burned.

Macon *Georgia Weekly Telegraph and Journal and Messenger*, March 16, 1875, p. 6. "The Court-house and an Entire Block Consumed," Columbus *Sunday Enquirer*, March 14, 1875, p. 2.

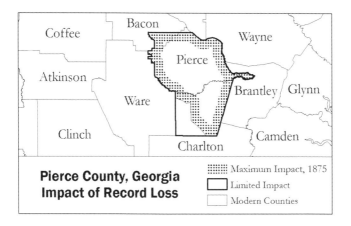

Pierce County, Georgia
Impact of Record Loss

::::: Maximum Impact, 1875
☐ Limited Impact
☐ Modern Counties

The courthouse and all other unoccupied buildings in Cedartown, seat of Polk County, were burned by U.S. military forces on November 1 or 2, 1864. The Fifteenth and Seventeenth corps entered the town during the middle of the day on November 1 and left by 7 a.m. the next morning. Almost all of the county's records survived the Civil War. Only the ordinary court minutes and administrators'

bonds were lost.

Despite being repeated in multiple twentieth-century sources, no contemporary evidence exists for a purported courthouse fire in 1887. Grand jury presentments make no mention of problems with the courthouse, and a destructive fire would not have been overlooked. In September 1888, the county commission decided to build a new courthouse with a budget of $20,000—a decision ridiculed by the *Rockmart Slate* newspaper. The contract was opened for bids by January 12, 1889 and the new building was finished by October 14, 1889.

Official Records, Armies, Ser. I, Vol. XXXIX, Pt. I, 733.

Official Records, Armies, Ser. I, Vol. XXXIX, Pt. III, 579, 597.

Tom Hightower to his Wife, November 28, 1864, New Market, Va., in Mills Lane (ed.), *"Dear Mother: Don't Grieve About Me. If I Get Killed, I'll Only be Dead.": Letters from Georgia Soldiers in the Civil War* (Savannah: Beehive Press, 1977), 337–338.

"From Rome," Macon *Daily Telegraph and Confederate*, December 7, 1864, p. 1.

Polk Co., Superior Court, Minutes, 1885–1889: 425–433, 480–483, 539–541.

Columbus *Enquirer-Sun*, September 18, 1888, p. 3.

"Cedartown is Building Up," Atlanta *Constitution*, January 12, 1889, p. 2.

"Future of Cedartown," Atlanta *Constitution*, October 14, 1889, p. 17.

Early in the morning of February 1, 1921, the Quitman County courthouse at Georgetown was destroyed by fire. The building was quickly consumed. Almost all of the county's records, dating back to 1858, were destroyed.

Quitman

"Quitman Courthouse Destroyed by Fire," Atlanta *Constitution*, February 2, 1921, p. 4.

"Quitman Court House Destroyed," Macon *Daily Telegraph*, February 2, 1921, p. 4.

Screven

The Screven County courthouse at Sylvania was destroyed during the Civil War, likely during Sherman's March to the Sea. The exact circumstances have not come to light, but divisions of the Twentieth Corps and Fourteenth Corps, along with cavalry regiments, passed through Sylvania from December 3 to 6, 1864. A replacement courthouse was built in 1869.

That building was destroyed almost thirty years later when Sylvania's business section burned. The fire started about 10 p.m. on January 8, 1897, in a livery stable. Within three hours, all the structures on the business block lay in ashes, including the courthouse. Many of Screven County's records have been lost over time. The widely varying starting dates of different records make it difficult to attribute losses to a particular event.

Official Records, Armies, Ser. I, Vol. XLIV, 372, 378, 609, 617, 628, 631, 789.
"Scriven County," Macon *Georgia Weekly Telegraph*, May 7, 1869, p. 1.
"Sylvania is Heavy Loser by Flames," Atlanta *Constitution*, January 9, 1897, p. 1.

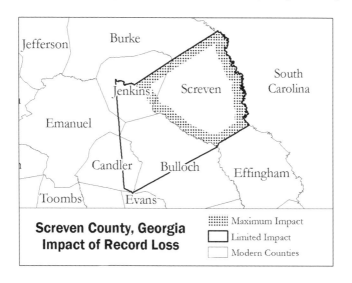

**Screven County, Georgia
Impact of Record Loss**

Maximum Impact
Limited Impact
Modern Counties

The temporary Seminole County courthouse at Donalsonville, along with all the books inside, was destroyed by fire in March 1922. The county had been created on November 2, 1920. Plans for the county's courthouse, which is still in use ninety years later, had been approved in January 1922 and construction bids were taken in March.

"Chase's Plans For Courthouse Are Approved," Atlanta *Constitution*, January 9, 1922, p. 5.
Georgia Laws, 1923, 909.

The Spalding County courthouse at Griffin was gutted by fire on January 12, 1981. A school teacher spotted flames coming out of the windows at about 9:30 p.m. The blaze swirled around the superior and probate courts, but—incredibly—the offices avoided damage and the county's records survived. An incident in February 1874, when hot bricks used to warm the clerk's feet set a fire, was caught before any serious damage happened.

"Georgia News," Columbus *Sun and Daily Enquirer*, February 7, 1874, p. 2.
"It's Death Spectacular," Griffin *Daily News*, January 13, 1981, p. 1.

The Stewart County courthouse at Lumpkin, which had been constructed in 1895, was destroyed by fire at 4 a.m. on April 21, 1922. The cause was not determined. Almost all of the county's records were stored in fireproof vaults and survived.

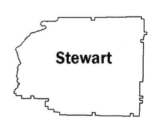

"Prey to Flames," Macon *Daily Telegraph*, April 22, 1922, p. 14.

In the afternoon of February 12, 1892, Talbot County's 62-year-old courthouse at Talbotton burned. The county's records were saved. Until the building was replaced, court was held in the opera house.

"The Courthouse Burned," Atlanta *Constitution*, February 13, 1892, p. 3.
"The Talbot Court House," Columbus *Enquirer-Sun*, February 13, 1892, p. 1.
"Talbot's Court House Burnt," Macon *Telegraph*, February 13, 1892, p. 1.

The Telfair County courthouse at McRae burned on February 10, 1934. Since it affected the town and county where Governor Eugene Talmadge had launched his political career, he was notified immediately. The fire

started in the roof of the courthouse. County records were stored in a fire-proof vault and survived, but the building was destroyed.

"Telfair Courthouse Destroyed by Blaze," Atlanta *Constitution*, February 11, 1934, p. 8B.

Early in the morning of November 21, 1917, the Toombs County courthouse at Lyons was completely destroyed. The county was only twelve years old. Its records were safe in vaults.

"Courthouse is Destroyed," Macon *Daily Telegraph*, November 22, 1917, p. 14.

An arsonist set fire to a first-floor phone booth in the Troup County courthouse at LaGrange just after 9 a.m. on the morning of November 5, 1936. Court business was underway and many people were in the building. As the fire spread, those on the second floor had no option but to leap to safety. Three people were injured.

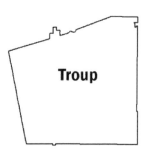

Some of the county commission records, which were being used at the time, burned. The county's other records were stored in a fire-proof vault and survived. Firemen had kept a steady stream of water on the vault.

"Troup County Courthouse Razed by LaGrange Fire," Atlanta *Constitution*, November 6, 1936, p. 1.

By 1901, Twiggs County's courthouse at Jeffersonville was one of the oldest in the state, having been built in 1825. It was a highly-worn wood frame building, with the courtroom on the first floor and offices on the second floor. It had been renovated only two years before. The courthouse had originally been built at Marion, but was moved after the Civil War when the county seat was changed to Jeffersonville.

At about 2 a.m. on the morning of February 7, 1901, the janitor at the county jail noticed flames coming through the roof of the courthouse. By then it was too late for anyone to save the structure. Although the courthouse contained two iron safes, they were not used for storing record books. Almost all of the county's records perished in the blaze, taking with them ninety-four years of history. The only item reported saved from the building was

Colonel L. D. Shannon's folding desk. He was the advisory counsel to the county board of commissioners.

"Court House Burned," Columbus *Enquirer-Sun*, February 8, 1901, p. 5.
"Twiggs' Courthouse Was Burned to the Ground," Macon *Telegraph*, February 8, 1901, p. 3.

The Walker County courthouse at Lafayette was set on fire about 2 a.m. the morning of February 2, 1883. The blaze destroyed the building along with almost all of the county's records, dating back fifty years. Multiple arson attempts over the following months

all targeted the county's records. The last known attack was made at the new courthouse about 1 a.m. on September 6, 1883, seven months after the old courthouse burned. That fire was discovered and extinguished almost as soon as it was started. All of the arson attempts were blamed on the same unknown person.

"Brief State Specials," Atlanta *Constitution*, February 3, 1883, p. 2.
Milledgeville *Union and Recorder*, February 6, 1883, p. 4.
"Trying to Destroy Records," New York *Times*, September 7, 1883, p. 1.

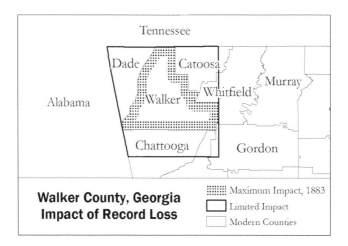

Walker County, Georgia Impact of Record Loss

Maximum Impact, 1883
Limited Impact
Modern Counties

Ware

On the night of October 12 and 13, 1874, the Ware County courthouse at Waycross was consumed by flames. The fire was set using kerosene. A nearby warehouse and store also caught fire, but quick action saved those buildings. The county's records, dating back to 1824, were almost completely lost.

Macon *Georgia Weekly Telegraph and Journal and Messenger*, October 20, 1874, p. 2.

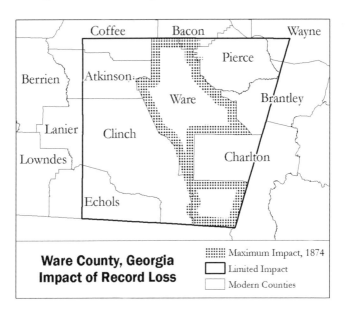

Ware County, Georgia
Impact of Record Loss

░░░ Maximum Impact, 1874
☐ Limited Impact
☐ Modern Counties

A fire broke out in the town of Warrenton, county seat of Warren County, at about 8 p.m. on April 23, 1854. It spread quickly through the downtown buildings, including the post office and courthouse. A shift in the wind and the onset of rain helped quell the blaze. The vast

Warren

majority of county records survived the destruction, although numerous deed books dating from 1817 to 1844 were lost.

Almost fifty-five years later, another fire in Warrenton destroyed the courthouse. It began in a kitchen about 10:30 p.m. on April 6, 1909, spread to an adjoining office and jumped to the courthouse. Fifty men and twenty-five women formed a bucket brigade, but the wood and brick building could not be saved. Water was carried from wells as much as a half mile away to stop the fire's progress. First reports that all the county's records were destroyed were inaccurate.

"Fire in Warrenton," Augusta *Daily Chronicle and Sentinel*, April 30, 1854, p. 2.
"Unchecked Flames Ravage Town; Warren Court House Is Consumed," Macon *Daily Telegraph*, April 7, 1909, p. 1.

The entire town of Sandersville, county seat of Washington County, burned March 24, 1855, including the courthouse. The fire started about 2 p.m. in Nathan Renfroe's wood shop on the edge of town and spread quickly, aided by high winds. Citizens could do little but watch as flames advanced. Many of the county records were removed from the courthouse to the offices of the *Central Georgian* newspaper, but that building also succumbed. The county lost almost all of its records.

The next courthouse was destroyed during the Civil War. Before leaving Sandersville at 9 a.m. on November 27, 1864, federal troops set fire to the building. General Sherman had ordered the destruction after Confederate defenders used the portico to fire on advancing troops. Probate records were saved, but the superior court's records were destroyed.

"Destructive Conflagration," Macon *Georgia Telegraph*, March 27, 1855, p. 2.
"Sandersville In Ruins," Milledgeville *Southern Recorder*, March 27, 1855, p. 2.
Official Records, Armies, Ser. III, Vol. IV, 400–402.

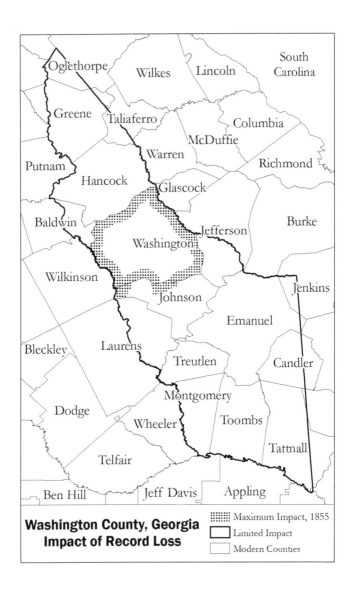

Washington County, Georgia
Impact of Record Loss

▦ Maximum Impact, 1855
☐ Limited Impact
☐ Modern Counties

Oglethorpe
Wilkes
Lincoln
South Carolina
Greene
Taliaferro
Columbia
McDuffie
Warren
Putnam
Richmond
Hancock
Glascock
Baldwin
Jefferson
Burke
Washington
Wilkinson
Johnson
Jenkins
Emanuel
Bleckley
Laurens
Treutlen
Candler
Dodge
Montgomery
Wheeler
Toombs
Tattnall
Telfair
Ben Hill
Jeff Davis
Appling

58

An arsonist set fire to the Webster County courthouse at Preston shortly before 10:45 p.m. on September 27, 1914. Kerosene was likely used to start the blaze, which originated at the foot of the main stairway leading to the upstairs courtroom. The fifty-nine-year-old wooden building was quickly consumed. The county's records suffered

heavy losses, although not all the books were destroyed.

"Webster Courthouse Destroyed by Flames," Atlanta *Constitution*, September 29, 1914, p. 9.

"Webster County Courthouse Burned Sunday Evening; Loss Complete," Americus *Weekly Times-Recorder*, October 1, 1914, p. 8.

On March 9, 1916, Wheeler County's new brick courthouse at Alamo was gutted by fire. The county had been formed less than four years earlier. Its records were saved.

"Wheeler Courthouse Is Gutted by Flames," Atlanta *Constitution*, March 11, 1916, p. 11.

An attempt to burn the Wilcox County courthouse at Abbeville was made on Friday, March 29, 1878, but the arsonist was foiled before the plan could be carried out. The person apparently returned, because the

next night—March 30 and 31, 1878—the building was successfully set on fire and destroyed. Many of the county's records have been lost, but the varying dates of early court books make it impossible to attribute particular losses to the 1878 fire.

"Georgia Press," Milledgeville *Union and Recorder*, April 2, 1878, p. 2.

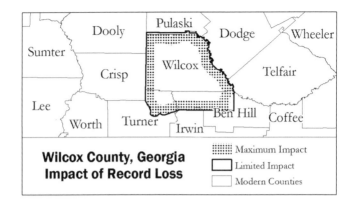

Wilcox County, Georgia
Impact of Record Loss

▦ Maximum Impact
☐ Limited Impact
☐ Modern Counties

Wilkes

Wilkes County's fifty-four-year-old courthouse at Washington was destroyed by fire on Christmas Eve, December 24, 1958. The cause was either faulty wiring or an overheated flue. The blaze could not be controlled, and it gutted the building, leading to the collapse of the roof. It started about 10:30 a.m., and the clock stopped an hour later. Except for papers in court offices, the county's records were protected in fire-proof vaults.

"Fire Guts Courthouse in Wilkes," Augusta *Chronicle-Herald*, December 25, 1958, sec. B, p. 6.

Fire destroyed the office of the Wilkinson County superior court at Irwinton on the evening of March 16, 1828. All of the records were lost. The structure was separate from the county courthouse, which was not affected.

An arsonist burned the courthouse about 10 p.m. on February 7, 1854. The building and its

Wilkinson

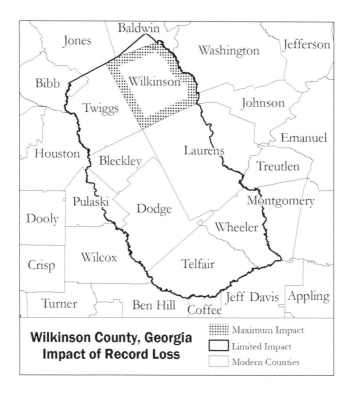

**Wilkinson County, Georgia
Impact of Record Loss**

▦ Maximum Impact
▢ Limited Impact
▢ Modern Counties

contents were destroyed. Two men were indicted, including the former clerk of superior court.

During the Civil War, the courthouse was destroyed by federal troops on their way to Savannah. Divisions of the Fifteenth Corps and Twentieth Corps began arriving in Irwinton late in the day on November 23, 1864, and by mid-morning November 26 most had continued their march.

The most recent fire occurred between 2:30 and 3 a.m. on the morning of February 15, 1924. Discovered by the sheriff, efforts to save the courthouse failed. First reports stated that most records were saved.

The four fires have wreaked havoc on the county's records. Deeds survive from 1854, and superior court minutes from 1864.

Very few probate records survived the Civil War. A significant number of late-19th century county records have been lost, likely attributable to the 1924 fire.

"Destructive Fire," Milledgeville *Southern Recorder*, March 17, 1828, p. 3.
Milledgeville *Southern Recorder*, February 14, 1854, p. 2.
"Burning of the Court-house in Irwinton," Milledgeville *Southern Recorder*, April 25, 1854, p. 3.
Official Records, Armies, Ser. I, Vol. XLIV, 529, 539, 544.
"New Court House in Wilkinson," Milledgeville *Federal Union*, May 18, 1869, p. 2.
"Irwinton Courthouse Destroyed by Flames," Augusta *Chronicle*, February 16, 1924, p. 3.

Worth County lost four of its courthouses to fire. On the night of January 26 and 27, 1879, an arsonist set fire to the courthouse at Isabella. The blaze quickly consumed the wood-frame building. All of the county's records, except one will book and some marriages, were destroyed. The law papers of attorney W. A. Harris, kept in his courthouse office, were also lost. Only a year and nine months later, the next courthouse also burned. The fire was discovered at about 10 p.m. on October 24, 1880. That time, the records survived in a new fire-proof safe.

The county lost a third courthouse early on August 9, 1893, at about 2 a.m. Arson was once again blamed. Some people believed the fire was set by someone who wished the county site be moved to Sylvester. Others speculated that it was caused by someone trying to evade prosecution. Only two superior court record books survived; the rest, including deeds, burned. Probate records escaped mostly unharmed.

The county seat was moved to Sylvester in 1904 and a new courthouse was finished the following year. That building became the fourth lost in Worth County when a fire was set in the sheriff's office about 2:45 a.m. on January 27, 1982. Ten months later, a jury convicted a 28-year-old man of arson in connection with the event. His goal had been to destroy drug evidence being used in the prosecution of a friend. The county's records had been microfilmed only four days prior to the fire.

"Burning of the Court-House in Worth County," Atlanta *Daily Constitution*, February 1, 1879, p. 4.

Milledgeville *Union and Recorder*, November 2, 1880, p. 1.

"Courthouse Burned," Atlanta *Constitution*, August 10, 1893, p. 2.

"Worth County Courthouse Destroyed," Marietta *Daily Journal*, January 28, 1982, p. 2.

"1 convicted of burning courthouse," Augusta *Chronicle*, November 12, 1982, p. 14A.

Worth County, Georgia
Impact of Record Loss

Maximum Impact
Limited Impact
Modern Counties

Index

Made in the USA
Columbia, SC
02 January 2020